Passive Income

Learn to Easily Make Passive Money Online and Quit Your Job! Utilize Multiple Income Streams to Pay Off Debt and Become Financially Free

Table of Contents

Introduction 3

Chapter 1: Passive Income 101 – the Basics 5

Chapter 2: Niche Websites 11

Chapter 3: Affiliate Marketing 16

Chapter 4: Email Marketing 21

Chapter 5: Amazon FBA 26

Chapter 6: Kindle Publishing 30

Chapter 7: Udemy – Creating Online Courses 34

Chapter 8: Drop Shipping 38

Chapter 9: YouTube – Making a Profit through Video Content 42

Conclusion 46

Introduction

I want to thank you and congratulate you for downloading the book *Passive Income: Learn to Easily Make Passive Money Online and Quit Your Job! Utilize Multiple Income Streams to Pay Off Debt and Become Financially Free.* You've made a fantastic decision to invest in your full earning potential by purchasing a great beginner's guide to earning passive income.

This book contains proven steps and strategies on how to truly take charge of your life. Are you tired of feeling directionless? Maybe you don't feel directionless, but rather feel unhappy with the direction in which you're currently going. After reading this book, there is no doubt that you will be able to begin earning money in ways that you may have never even considered. As the internet continues to grow, so does the ability to make money through it! The tips in this book are crucial to understanding the fundamentals on how to begin this priceless process.

If you have little to no idea of where to start, don't panic. This book will be your guide to acquiring everything you need both internally and externally about how to make money online, even when you're not physically working. With this capability, you'll be able to spend more time doing the things you love and less time worrying about your next paycheck. This book, while it will discuss exactly how to begin earning passive income, such as through Kindle e-book publishing and Amazon FBA, will also discuss the subtler aspects of being able to successfully start a passive income outlet, like how to understand the risks involved and what your mindset should be like as you begin to think more like a businessman or woman and less like a customer.

Here's an inescapable fact: you will need patience, energy, time, and enthusiasm in order to have what it takes to begin earning passive income. It's an unavoidable truth that some real dedication and work is necessary prior to becoming successful in this arena. In addition to putting in the right amount of effort, it is equally important for you to understand that it takes time to grow any type of business, even one that does not necessarily need the owner's active participation in order to make money. If you can combine these four features, you'll be kicking your feet up in no time while you watch the cash roll in.

If you do not develop your understanding of how to begin earning passive income, you will forever be in lust of finding supplemental income for yourself. You will always be chasing the dream of having more money, but you won't have taken any action to actualize your goals. There is always going to be an excuse that you can make for yourself – that you don't have the time, or the money, or you don't think you're smart enough. Why wait? You have made a great choice for yourself by downloading this book. The time to take advantage of the voluminous ways to make money on the internet is now! Who knows, one day you might even make enough money with the passive income strategies presented in this book that you'll be able to quit the job you currently have.

There is no time to waste in figuring out how to start earning a living on your terms. It's time for you to become an amazing entrepreneur and passive income earner! Let's get started!

Chapter 1:
Passive Income 101 – the Basics

If you've ever felt overwhelmed by the number of bills that you have or the amount of debt that's piling up in one of your credit card accounts, you're not alone. People everywhere are constantly struggling to make ends meet. Half the time it seems like the bills are endless; car insurance, home owner's insurance, food for the week, pet supply bills, the list goes on. Just as you feel like you have caught up, that maybe you can bury some of your next paycheck away into a savings account, the dishwasher breaks or your car engine goes bust. Wouldn't it be nice, luxurious really, if you had supplemental income that you didn't have to spend time earning? Instead of getting a part time job to make ends meet, this money would manifest automatically when people chose to interact with a good or service you were providing remotely. This type of supplemental income situation may seem like a dream, but it's a dream that so many people have contemplated that it's become a reality. This type of earning is collectively known as passive income.

What is Passive Income?

Most commonly, passive income is defined as income that can be earned in one of two ways. The first is when an individual owns part of or all of a business, but does not actively participate in the day-to-day processes of that business in order to make money (he or she "passively" participates, get the name?) This type of ownership includes royalties on a book or music venture or owning stock in in a company that pays dividends. The second way that an individual can earn passive income is through the ownership of an investment property. This is when an individual owns a property, but he or she is renting it out to other people and a profit is being generated through renting the space. Instead of having to spend a majority of his or her money on rent, the owner of the property reaps the reward of being able to use the money from the rent towards the mortgage. This frees up income for the property owner without much effort on his or her end.

Passive income provides a great way to supplement income that you're already earning without the time commitment that's attached to a full time job. Imagine if you were to combine a couple of different ways to earn passive income. The possibility exists that over time it would not be necessary to have a typical day job. While the prime advantages to creating streams of passive income include getting paid while you're on vacation or visiting some remote place, without taking crucial steps and thinking about your business ventures in a certain way, your grand idea for making passive income could turn out to be one giant flop. Let's look at what your mindset should be as your brain begins to turn its wheels towards developing passive income revenue streams. If you don't understand how you should be thinking about this type of business venture, success will be less likely.

Mindset Tip 1: What is Your Current Life Cycle?

The first important question to ask yourself before jumping into earning passive income is to ask yourself what type of life cycle you are currently in. For example, are you a single mother with two kids, or are you married with no kids and are benefitting from your income in addition to income from your spouse. Analyzing how you are currently making money will help you understand where your money is currently going and how your income affects the livelihood of your family. It's understood by most economists who focus on spending habits that people are generally consistent in their saving habits over the course of a life. While your life cycle is slowly changing over time (you won't be single forever, you might have children someday, etc.) it's important to notice for yourself how you deal with saving, spending, and earning based on what your personal situation currently is.

Why Do You Want Passive Income?

In addition to understanding your personal economic dynamics within the broader scheme of your familial setup, another important question to ask yourself is why you want to start earning passive income. Sure, most of us could use an extra thousand here or there, but when you ask yourself this question, it's not enough to simply want more money. There should be a category for where you want this money to go. For example, an adequate answer is if you have some credit card debt and you think that earning passive income could be a great way to get rid of it in a timely manner. Another example of an adequate response is that you are looking to take a class to learn woodworking, or any hobby or sport that you would like to learn more about, but you don't want to use your current source of income for this endeavor. It's important to realize that if you answer this question by stating that you don't feel like you're earning enough money at your current job, it might be more beneficial for you to look for a new type of career, not as a way to earn passive income. Passive income should be *supplemental*, and should at no point be considered the more preferential way to earn money or the way that will "save" you financially. Consider this before doing anything rash.

Asking yourself what type of life cycle you're currently in and also why you really are looking for ways to make passive income are two crucial places to start when first considering passive income as an option. After you've asked yourself these questions and have taken time to ponder your answers (maybe you make a list for yourself in each category), you are still not ready to start earning passive income just yet. There are other considerations you should be making in order to make sure that this is an endeavor you wish to embark on. There are two common misconceptions that people make about earning passive income. They are outlined here because sometimes people have delusions about what earning passive income is truly like. Let's take a look at these two major types of misunderstandings now.

1. "Make Money While You Sleep"

   The ability to make money while you sleep is a mantra that's often touted during discussions about making money through earning passive income. A lot of people think that when someone decides to seek earning passive income, that he or she is basically luckier than the average human being and that almost no work is involved in getting a passive business off of the ground. This is simply not sure. In the beginning, developing a way to receive passive income is hard work. There is no other way to describe it. It doesn't matter which type of passive income you're pursuing. The reality is that it is likely you will receive little to no compensation until the processes of your business plan have been fully configured and implemented into an online space. It doesn't matter if you plan to start a blog, or invest in peer-to-peer lending, or develop a place for yourself in the Kindle marketplace. All of these avenues take time to set up, and research is involved in planning to make your success inevitable. This is especially true if you are planning to develop an automated service such as offering an online course. While eventually you will have the capability to be more hands off with a business like this, getting the material prepared to sell online takes time and effort. If you don't set out to develop your business the right way from the start, you may run into the problem of having to stop doing business due to poor planning and customer dissatisfaction. Take the time in the beginning to plan your business out entirely. Remember that passive income requires work, at least in the beginning, and remember that passive income does not necessarily mean passive effort or workload. Keep this in mind and you will thank yourself later.

2. Identify Risk When You See It

If there were no risks involved with developing a way to earn passive income, more people would choose to earn money this way. While the startup costs in general may be greater in one type of earning than in another, the time spent developing these processes should not be understated. Some people, while he or she may need more money, but do not have enough time to earn money this way. If you have kids, or already have a second job, or work long hours at your current job, this may not be the avenue for you. There are risks involved in starting any new venture, as well as money that needs to be invested into these methods up front in order for success to occur. For all of the strategies that we will go through in the following chapters, risk is involved in every one. Additionally, if the product you are selling your customers is subpar or does not speak to a need that he or she has, the risk of investing in earning passive income will outweigh the reward over time. Countering the possibilities of risk require research in the field in which you're going to enter, energy on your part to make sure all ground is covered, and most importantly making sure that you have sufficient funds to embark on earning passive income. Be aware of the risks before investing in anything. Broadly speaking, it is important to always keep this in mind. Before you set out to earn passive income, make sure that you aware of the specific risks involved.

Once you have asked yourself key questions such as, "What type of life cycle am I currently in?" and, "Why do I want to earn passive income?" and you feel that you have a real understanding of the effort and risk involved, it is time to start planning exactly how you will make your cash. Will you earn money by selling courses that you've created online, or do you have more of a knack for blogging for profit? Maybe instead, you have dreams of becoming a YouTube sensation. While this chapter focused on the extremely basic parameters of passive income, the next chapters will look at specific markets and provide you with tips on how to profit within these respective fields.

Chapter 2:
Niche Websites

While blogging seems to be the new fad for anyone with a computer and some writing skills, it can be tough to make money solely from this type of platform. Blogs require time to build a fan base and regular readership, and if you as the blogger are not aware of what needs to be done on your blog site that can generate more viewers and clicks to your page, the blog that you hoped would take off and make you money will most likely only amount to being the equivalent of a diary or a journal. Without targeting your message and optimizing your words so that people see your content, it will be hard to get many people visiting your site. Instead of strictly making a blog that ranges in what it's subject matter is, what if you narrowed your subject matter and targeted questions that people have or sought to explain how to fix problems for others. This is what a niche website is all about.

What is a Niche Website?

A niche website is a website that seeks to target a small group of people within a larger category of interest. Its goal is to offer the reader valuable content that addresses the answer to a question or solves a problem. The owner of the website does this by finding a keyword or phrase that people Google often. The keyword or phrase is chosen by the niche website by making sure that the current needs that people have surrounding this keyword or phrase are not being met in the best way possible. To explain this, we will use the example of a sports website. If an individual wanted to create a niche website dedicated to sports, he or she would not simply post articles related to all types of sports. Instead, he or she would select a very specific aspect of sports to write about and promote. For example, instead of choosing to write about golf, tennis and swimming all in one week, a niche website would be dedicated to only discussing swimming; however, not just the subject of swimming as a whole. The owner of the site narrows the topic of swimming even further, maybe dedicating the site to offering resources for swim lessons for kids throughout the country or creating an entire website that is dedicated to providing tips on how to master a stroke such as butterfly or breaststroke. Through this example, it is easy to see how a niche website targets a subset of the larger market. The narrower the subset can be, the better.

It seems like it would make more sense for an individual to target the entire swimming market, but the competition within this huge market is what makes this approach not-recommended. Think about other sites that you are competing against within the swimming category. Websites that are owned by Speedo and other companies that have a certain monopoly on swimming are the types of websites that would drown your site and make it irrelevant. These companies have an endless amount of resources that they can apply that will guarantee that their site consistently ranks at the top of the Google search engine. By narrowing your keywords to include something specific that only a small subset of the swimming population will search, you are giving yourself more of an opportunity to be the "expert" within that subset. This will help to ensure that the people who are googling your keywords are getting to your site first, because your site is the most informative regarding the particular subject and keyword phrase that you have chosen.

Now that we know what the possibilities of a niche site are, let's look at how to successfully create one.

Step 1 to Creating a Niche Site: Brainstorm ideas

The first step in creating a niche site is to brainstorm ideas about what your niche site will be about. When doing this, it might be beneficial to think about topics that you personally find interesting. Why would you want to write about something that you find boring or have to spend a lot of time researching? Because this is still the brainstorming stage, the ideas do not have to be formal or "right". Get creative, and be as specific as possible. If you have a broad topic in mind, use this brainstorming time to break down your topic smaller and smaller until you are left with a topic that people want to learn more about.

Step 2 to Creating a Niche Site: Pick Your Topic

After you've brainstormed all of the ideas you can think of regarding which website you're going to create, figure out which niche you're going to target based on what is the most profitable. This step will take some research into the world of SEO, Search Engine Optimization. Firstly, you want to make sure that the keywords you are choosing for your site have low competition and high volume. This means that a lot of people are googling what your site is going to offer and there are not many sites that are offering answers to their questions. If we go back to the example of swimming, this would mean picking the keyword phrase, "swimming butterfly" because your site is going to be specifically focusing on the stroke butterfly. There are some resources that can help you figure out your keywords. These include keyword analysis tools such as Market Samurai and Google AdWords, which inform you of which keywords are popular in a given field. It can prove difficult to find keywords that are not competitively being targeted by other niche sites yet still have a high volume of users searching for the content, so this process may take some time. Remember to be flexible when deciding on a niche topic.

Step 3 to Creating a Niche Site: Set Up Your Site

Once you have a definitive topic in mind and you know that there is potential for it to yield a high volume of traffic to your site, it's finally time to physically create your site. The best advice that can be given in this section is to set up your site for as cheaply as possible. Luckily for you, creating a niche site is one of the cheaper ways to make passive income. The first step is to purchase a domain name. In the United States, domain names run for about $15.00 on average, with the more expensive domain names costing $35.00 and the cheaper one's costing $10.00. Services like Google Domains and GoDaddy.com can help you easily register your name. The domain name will be active for a year, at which point you have the option of renewing or discontinuing your service. Don't be discouraged if your dream domain name is already in use. It's okay to have a domain name that doesn't perfectly match with your topic. Again, be creative and flexible. The alternative to being flexible is to get into a bidding war over a domain name with someone who owns the rights to it. If you want to keep your costs to a minimum, avoid bargaining for the perfect domain name.

Once you have a domain name, find a site to host you. While the domain name and the host site work together, it might be beneficial for you to use the same source for the domain name and the host site. A host site is a site that finds space for your web page within the internet, and this cyber-property averages around $6.00 per month to maintain. This is a pretty straightforward step.

Next, start creating content for your site that is valuable. Online writing is not entirely about an article's literate value, it's also about presentation. Some easy ways to jumpstart your niche site is to write five posts that focus on reviewing the most popular products in your niche at the time. This will easily drive people to your site when they are looking for information or reviews on a specific piece of merchandise. Tutorials can also drive users to your page. A good goal to reach is to post at least three well-written tutorials to your website shortly after it goes live. Lastly, seek to write at least five list posts for your site that speaks to promoting your niche. For example, if your topic is swimming, you can post a list about what the best gifts are to give swimmers during the holidays. These lists, while they're easy to write, also present people with the opportunity to share them with others on social media platforms, like Facebook or post a URL on Twitter that links back to your original post.

Remember, it might take time for your site to gain traction. Be patient during your research phase and while you're waiting to see monetary results. As you can see, it takes a lot of work to start a niche website, but if you follow these steps, you will eventually begin to see some profit. Additionally, some other tips to consider while trying to promote your site is to build an email list, promote your website by telling your friends about it and building social media platforms for it. Also reach out to the people within your niche who seem to be most successful in the industry. It can never hurt to communicate with people who share a similar interest with you, and if you can find a way for them to promote your site, you and your niche website will be in a great position.

Chapter 3:
Affiliate Marketing

Let's make up a scenario where you love waffles. You love them so much that you don't buy them in the grocery store, because you eat them so quickly that you're always running out. Instead, you purchase the waffles in bulk on Amazon because they're cheaper this way (you make sure to have them shipped overnight, so they don't go bad). Stay with me here. It turns out that you also have recently launched your niche website, and instead of swimming for this chapter you have decided to dedicate your site to specifically how to make the best waffles. Because of this, you decide to reach out to your vendor from Amazon and negotiate a deal where you post ads about the waffles they sell to your site. Every time a customer who is visiting your site clicks on the ad for the waffles and buys from the Amazon vendor, you get a commission from the sale. Sounds great, right? This is an example that demonstrates affiliate marketing at work.

If the waffle example above still hasn't completely ironed out a firm definition for you, affiliate marketing is an online form of advertising where one business compensates another business to promote it. One way to think of this is to compare affiliate marketing to a salesperson who only gets paid on commission. Before looking at the steps to take to become involved in affiliate marketing, it is important to discuss some general guidelines to follow before immersing yourself into this promotional vehicle. While this can be a great way to generate money on your site, there are ways to implement this strategy that are more useful than others. Let's look at some general recommended techniques for when using affiliate marketing. A precursor to this, which may sound redundant but should be explained, is that you need to own a website in order to implement these affiliate marketing strategies. If you need a quick refresher on this, head back to chapter 1 before reading further.

Tip 1: How to Choose the Products You Promote

A good general rule to begin with when choosing to engage in affiliate marketing is to set some sort of moral compass and only promote products that you actually find useful to fixing some sort of discomfort in your life. When you promote products that you really do find value in, they are easier to promote and you are being honest with your readership. If you are not confident in the product's ability to better someone's life, don't promote it. While you may find yourself confronted with the temptation to promote product's with which you're unfamiliar, especially if you are having a hard time gaining ground with products that you would love to promote, have some patience. Don't promote a product simply because the opportunity is there.

Tip 2: Telling Versus Recommending

It has been proven that affiliate marketing is more successful when the affiliate website does not directly tell their customer to buy the product they're promoting. Instead, the affiliate site should seek to recommend the product to its customer based on his or her experience with the product, preferably within the context of the purpose of the site on which the product is being promoted. For example, it would be easy to promote waffles that you've been buying off of Amazon on your waffle-making website because you love the product and truly believe that all palates would benefit from tasting this scrumptious waffle goodness. Because you have personally experienced the product in question, a better way to promote it, rather than simply saying, "buy this now", would be to explain your experience with the product and emphasize why the product should be bought.

Now that you are aware of some general guidelines for how to attack affiliate marketing, it's time to look at exactly what how affiliate marketing works and where to begin.

How an Affiliate Program Works

While we will discuss ways to find a good affiliate program later in this section, you first need to understand how they work. Upon entering an affiliate program, the seller will provide you with computer programming code that refers clickable traffic on your site back to their website. These codes primarily manifest themselves through banners that promote the seller and text links that get embedded into your website's literature. Software is available to the seller that allows the business to track your performance, and you will most likely be given an affiliate ID as well. It is up to the seller which software platform he or she will use, but this will also give you, the affiliate, the opportunity to receive real-time statistics on your sales and commissions for a specific product. These techniques may vary slightly depending on specific affiliate guidelines within a company's structure. This gives you a broad overview of how a program will work. Additionally, there are three different ways a seller can opt to pay an affiliate:

1. Pay Per Lead: You're paid when your reader fills out contact information on the seller's website.

2. Pay Per Click: You're paid when your reader clicks on the ad for the seller's site, regardless of whether or not the reader buys the seller's product.

3. Pay Per Sale: You're paid only when your reader buys the seller's product from the seller's site.

Each payment type has its own advantages and disadvantages. Be sure to understand what type of deal your affiliate program offers before committing.

A List of Affiliate Programs

In addition to understanding how affiliate programs work in general, it is equally important to note that each one operates slightly different. Each one has nuances to it that you should understand before contacting one. Don't be intimidated when trying to find a reputable affiliate program. Some great affiliate programs to research and check out include the following:

- Google AdSense
- Amazon Associates
- ShareASale
- ClickBank
- LinkShare

Be sure to research each affiliate program, especially when deciding on which products to promote. Amazon in particular offers great ways to get insight on which products are most popular in your niche, and this is a valuable resource when deciding on which products you want to promote. The biggest advantage to affiliate marketing is its cost effectiveness. You don't have to worry about creating a product because the seller had already done that for you. You also don't have to hire employees. This is a great method to implement if you already have a website and are looking for a way to make some passive income with relatively low starting costs.

Chapter 4:
Email Marketing

Everyone hates spam. More than ever before, it can seem like every relevant online company has an email marketing campaign, and you are subscribed to every single one of them. An inbox can fill from zero to hundreds of emails overnight, and most of these emails contain ways to motivate your wallet towards empty. Can you imagine if you were to give in to all of the messages that populate your inbox? It's safe to say you could spend a lot of money in a short amount of time. Nevertheless, these days an email marketing campaign is a must for anyone who is serious about growing a business. If you can grow your email marketing strategies enough so that you begin to see revenue from them, passive income is possible through this avenue.

How to Grow Your List of Email Subscribers

As a consumer, it can get a bit irritating to be constantly asked to provide your email address, especially when nothing is offered in return. It's gotten to the point where it's not uncommon to be asked your email address when you're at the register in a store buying a product. There's no explanation as to why the employee is prompted to ask you for it, and it can be a little uncomfortable to decline giving it out. Similarly, people are generally hesitant about giving out their email address online. While there is no sales representative physically in front of you on the web, it can still be irritating to be constantly prompted to provide an email address when there is no exchange of reward.

A great way to circumvent this problem is to offer free information or discounts to the customer on your website in exchange for his or her email address. This is the first step to gaining entry into an individual's coveted inbox so that you can compete with the rest of advertisers and merchants who have already arrived. While it's never too late to subscribe to the inbox competition, it is important that if you are going to compete that your emails get read. Let's look at some ways that you can give "stuff" away for free so that your customers will learn to trust you and not delete your message along with the rest of the junk that accrues in his or her inbox.

Consider Why Your Product Matters

The way to get to someone's money is not through describing the product's features, but rather by explaining the benefits through which a product can enhance an individual's life. If we look at the example of our waffle business again, we can see this concept in action. If you were to give away information on how to make the perfect waffle, you probably would not entice your potential customer to give you his or her email address by telling them that you can give them the fluffiest waffles or the waffles with the perfect crispiness. The amount of fluff and crisp of the waffle are *features* of the product. While these aspects of waffles are great, they will not grip your potential customer. All your customer wants to know is how can they benefit? What is it about the product that will improve his or her life? Copywriting principles are great to apply here, and another way to look at this is to ask, "So what?" when considering how to market your product or service via email. Why does your product matter to your customer?

Instead of talking about features, talking about benefits will give you much more success. For example, if instead of promising your customer free information on how to get the fluffiest waffle, offer information on how to make a waffle that will bring a family around the breakfast table on Sunday morning or a recipe for a waffle that saves a mother time. Creating family memories around your product and saving time are motivating benefits that can trigger the real reason why someone would be interested in your product. If a customer sees a benefit that you can provide instead of a feature, he or she is more likely to willingly provide you with an email address.

Combine Email Marketing with Affiliate Marketing

If you don't have actually have a product that you're offering and your website is more blog-like in nature than product-oriented, consider combining the techniques from chapter 3 about affiliate marketing with email marketing tactics. If you can generate a sound email following, the next step is to sell products as an affiliate directly from your email platform. Depending on how your affiliate program is organized, you could potentially get paid each time a consumer simply clicks on a link within your email that takes he or she to your seller's website. This is a fantastic way to earn passive income because it does not require that you yourself sell a product. This way, most of your attention can be on perfecting your email marketing strategies.

In addition to combining affiliate marketing with your email marketing, consider delineating your email list between those who are buying the products you are promoting and those who are not. For example, if you have a list of email addresses who are consistently buying what you are selling, you know that these people to be loyal customers. Send emails out to these people that upsell what they've already purchased.

The Importance of an Autoresponder

Another pet peeve that anyone who owns an email account can relate to is getting emails too frequently or infrequently. If a company is sending emails daily, this can drive a consumer to block an email account or sentence the business to spend the rest of its days in spam folder purgatory. Services like MailChimp and Aweber make it possible to schedule when you want your emails to be sent out. Participating with an autoresponder service is the perfect way to make sure that you're targeting the desires of your email subscribers without feeling like you have to be constantly watching over your email messages. Another good tip to use when sending out emails is to personalize your greeting to include the name of every individual who subscribes to your email thread. Services like Groupmail make this possible by offering a mail merge option that customizes each email to the person whom you're emailing. While this may seem like a miniscule detail, people are more likely to respond positively to your message if he or she feels like you are speaking directly to them.

Similar to the techniques found in affiliate marketing, email marketing strategies are largely cost effective while also being passive. While it might double your chances of making more sales if you combine affiliate marketing strategies with email marketing, be careful how quickly you adopt this approach. If you are just starting out, it might be more beneficial to start with one tactic and slowly integrate the other. Once you have a significant number of email subscribers, have your message tailored to target the benefits that you can offer your customers instead of your product's features, and have found an autoresponder service that works for you, you'll be seeing revenue through the tools that email marketing can provide in no time.

Chapter 5:
Amazon FBA

If you currently produce a product or service for online use, you know that the customer service aspect of the business can sometimes be exhausting. Not only do you have to keep your customers happy by answering any and all questions that might arise during your interaction, but you also have to package their goods correctly so that they arrive to the customer intact. With Fulfillment by Amazon (FBA), Amazon promises to take care of the headache surrounding your product for you. Amazon (FBA) is unlike the other types of passive income that we've previously discussed because there is more controversy over how profitable this type of passive income stream actually is. Here we will discuss how Amazon FBA works and how you can best navigate these practices. Depending on what you are planning on selling, you may or may not want to pursue this type of passive income.

Amazon FBA in a Nutshell

The first step to be involved with Amazon FBA is to create an FBA account with Amazon. That's easy enough, especially if you are already selling on Amazon now. The next step is to put your products up for sale on Amazon's website. You can either sell your own products (products that you've made) or you can act as a reseller and sell new and unused goods. As with the other ways to make passive income, this might require some research beforehand. For example, maybe you know that there are purses on sale at your local mall this week. So you would go to the mall, buy six purses, and then post them to Amazon in your selling portal. In the section of the portal where it says, "Fulfilled by", it typically states that the Seller (You) are the person fulfilling the order; however, because you have made yourself an FBA account, you have the option of instead choosing Amazon to fulfill the order for you.

It costs $39.99 per month to use Amazon FBA. This does not include additional fees that will be taken from you after your product is sold and shipped. Before doing anything else, you should make sure that you want to spend $39.99 on this service, and make sure that your business can afford it. Once you have opted for Amazon to fulfill the order, you "Create your Shipment"; this means that you're sending your order to Amazon. Amazon requires you to send your product a certain way, so you have to make sure to follow the specific FBA guidelines. This ensures that the Amazon customer will have a great experience. Amazon gives you the option of the either correctly labeling your shipments yourself, or Amazon will do this for you for a fee. Additionally, if your shipments are all of a similar category and are all newly purchased, you can ship them all together in one box (obviously this won't work if you are making the product yourself). This saves you money on packaging resources. While shipping still does cost you money, Amazon guarantees that it will be heavily discounted.

From your customer's perspective, if you link with Amazon FBA, Prime members will receive free shipping on products that you sell. For you, the seller, if you have another online store in addition to Amazon's, Amazon enables you to use your Amazon inventory for your customers from other platforms. This gives you the flexibility what you want with your merchandise. It also stresses a point about Amazon FBA; once you send your goods to them, the product is still yours. Think of it as if you owned a giant warehouse. If at any point you need the merchandise for another venture, you're able to take it. In a way, you're giving your merchandise the flexibility to populate two marketplaces at once. To some sellers, this is a huge advantage. Lastly, Amazon gives you the option of setting your selling preferences in a way that uses their application program interface (API) the control to generate transactions for you. Obviously, this is the most hands-off option available for a seller who is using Amazon FBA.

Advantages and Disadvantages to Using Amazon FBA

For this type of venture to be most advantageous to you, you should be someone who is making the product yourself or who is buying products to be sold online. If you're looking for products to re-sell, it is crucial that you find discounts at your local stores and sell products that are all in one pre-authorized category so that they can be shipped together. If you're selling products that you're making yourself, Amazon FBA allows you to create multiple platforms for your product from which people can look at it.

Contrastingly, a disadvantage that Amazon FBA does not directly mention to its users is that there is potential for your business to develop a bad reputation because of the way in which Amazon FBA works. For example, when items are co-mingled into similar categories and shipped out, there is potential for a customer who ordered your particular good to receive the same good but whom someone else gave to Amazon FBA. This is due to the fact that Amazon sends items to their customers based on locational convenience, not necessarily based on which seller sent the item. If we go back to the example of a purse, let's say that you sent Amazon a real Coach purse to sell online. The purse you sent was truly manufactured by Coach. Another seller sent Amazon the same purse, except that it is counterfeit and he or she is selling it online as real. If someone were to purchase the purse online through you, and Amazon decided to send your customer the counterfeit purse because it was being stored in a warehouse that was closer to the customer than where your purse was, your customer would be angry with you once he or she received the purse and realized it was counterfeit. The potential exists for this customer to post negative reviews on your selling page, and if this happened it could affect your sales in the future. People are less likely to buy goods from you if it looks like you are trying to cheat them.

　　While people have made gobs of money by using Amazon FBA, it is important to consider why you want to use the service before committing. If you find shipping and customer service to be a nightmare, this service might be a good fit for you, and there is potential to make a profit from it. It is widely known that Amazon FBA participants are usually more profitable when he or she spends more money with Amazon. When using Amazon FBA, there seems to be a positive correlation between spending and earning.

Chapter 6:
Kindle Publishing

Arguably one of the easiest ways to make passive income is through Kindle e-book publishing. Amazon gives the author seventy percent of the profit when a book sells, making this an advantageous adventure for many people with passive income interests. With the startup costs being cheap, this avenue that still indirectly relies on Amazon may be more advantageous to the novice passive income earner. Don't worry if you do not consider yourself to be the best writer. As a Kindle publisher, you can make a profit without writing any of the books yourself. Best of all, because these books are digital, they will be available for online purchase indefinitely. Let's go through the process of how to become a Kindle publisher.

Researching your Niche

Again, just as we saw in chapter 1 with the development of niche websites, similar research is involved when planning what topics to write an e-book on. Obviously you want your book to sell, and part of ensuring that it will is by having an awareness of what types of books customers desire. The first step is to pick a niche topic to write on. Figuring out which niche to target can be done pretty simply by looking at the Kindle bestseller list. Once you have figured out broadly which niche you want to write about based on what is popular, try to narrow your subject matter based on what is not being addressed in these books. For example, a good idea is to research the Kindle bestsellers by looking at the reviews of each book. If you see a negative review, or something that the customer states he or she would like additional information on, take note of it. The information within the reviews could be your starting point for writing on a topic within a broader niche that has not yet been addressed or has only been minimally written about so far. Additionally, as with niche websites, make sure that you are also looking at keywords that are being searched on the Kindle website. These keywords should be incorporated into your book, probably in the title.

Getting the Kindle Book Written

After you've decided on some niche topics that you'd like to write about, the next decision you have to make is deciding on who is going to write the books for you. If you decide to write the books yourself, it will be impossible to consider your endeavors as passive income. Writing a book takes time, and you not only want to write a book that is written efficiently, but you also want to make sure that it's edited properly. This will avoid the potential for dissatisfied customers. If Amazon is taking thirty percent of your Kindle e-book profit, and if you put your e-book on sale for $3.00, you are making $2.10 each time your book sells. If we take this example and consider the possibility that ten e-books are going to be sold in a week, that's $21.00 income earned per week. $21.00 on its own is not that much money. If you were to write these books yourself, you might be able to generate two books a week, which would maybe bring your profit to $42.00 per week instead of $21.00; however, with a good e-book being between thirty to sixty pages, you might find yourself swamped after a few weeks of publishing. Especially if you want Kindle book writing to be a second or third source of income, this type of dedication will surely prove unsustainable eventually.

A potentially better option for you, as the publisher, is to outsource people to write your e-books for you. Instead of writing two books per week, you can hire people to write e-books for you, making it possible to produce more books per week. Instead of writing two books per week, you might be able to produce five to ten books per week. If we look at our previous example and five books sell ten times in one week at $3.00 per book, your income jumps from $42.00 per week to $105 dollars per week. Depending on how many book writers you find, producing five books per week may eventually grow to producing ten books per week. The income potential exists based on the harder you work at researching good niches to target. It's up to you to find the topics, and up to your writers to produce the content.

A competitive rate for an e-book writer is $2.00 per 100 words of text, and when you are first starting your business you might even be able to find writers who will do this work for cheaper. A good place to look for writers is Upwork. Upwork is an application where freelance writers compete for jobs. As an employer, you are looking for the freelancer who will produce acceptable content for you at a reasonable price. If you were to pay someone to write a book for you at a rate of $1.00 per 100 words, a sixty-page book that you want written would cost you roughly two-hundred and forty dollars. If you look at the potential selling profitability of a single book, even after Amazon takes their cut, your profit margin could be around $800 over time. Of course, if you're not an illustrator, you would also have to pay someone to create a cover page for your book too. Paying someone to create a cover page for an e-book averages around $25.00.

An even bigger reason to consider looking into Kindle publishing is if you already own a niche website. Within an e-book, there is potential for you to link your website into the conclusion of the book and possibly generate email addresses from readers this way. Once you have a substantial amount of email addresses, you can use the affiliate marketing strategies from chapter 3 to link your e-books with your affiliate program. This way, you are generating income from two different sources, all within the Kindle publishing network.

Chapter 7:
Udemy – Creating Online Courses

If you're lucky enough to find that your niche market is also a personal passion for you, you might want to look into selling online courses on a given subject. This is particularly true if you're looking to sell a service rather than a product. In contrast to the previous chapter that focused on Amazon Kindle publishing, creating a course takes longer to produce, but you are also able to charge a lot more money once the course is created and complete. While there is still keyword-niche research that has to be done, good advice to follow is to look for a topic that is super specific that you can teach about. It needs to be a niche that not many people are searching for (between 500 to 2,000 searches), but a topic that these people are eager to learn a lot more about. While the process of creating an online course takes a considerable amount of time and energy, the end result is being able to charge your students large amounts to enjoy the content that you are going to teach. A great online course forum that allows you to upload your course to their site cheaply is Udemy. Let's take a look at what Udemy offers.

Publishing a Course on Udemy

Udemy is defined as an M.O.O.C website. This stands for massively-open online course. At this point in time, there are over ten million students who are taking classes on Udemy, and the site offers over forty-thousand courses. These statistics alone prove that for someone who is selling an online course, it makes sense to use Udemy because the customers are already concentrated in one place. While Udemy does offer free courses, courses that cost money range from $50.00

to as little as $20.00. While none of the courses on Udemy are currently eligible to be the equivalent of a college credit, many students on Udemy are looking to improve a job-related skill or skills in other areas of life. For example, Udemy has categories for beauty and makeup, home improvement, and pet training. As the creator of a course, this gives you a wide range of areas to choose from when deciding on which course to write about.

The Importance of Marketing

So, how much money can you make through Udemy? While Udemy offers the course creator basically a marketplace where he or she can sell coursework, there is obviously a fee attached; however, the fee is entirely reasonable. Udemy keeps 50% tuition of any student they bring to the course through their marketing efforts. You keep 100% of the profit for any student that you bring to your course through the Udemy platform. It is entirely free to put a course on Udemy. The marketing aspect of it is what can serve to make the seller of a course maximally profitable. It is important to start marketing your course for Udemy before it goes live. Let's look at some top tips to take note of from a marketing perspective that can easily set you apart from the rest of the courses on Udemy.

Top Tip 1: Talk to People Around You

Prior to creating a course, it's important to generate an awareness of what people would invest their money in to learn about. Simple ways that you can ask people about their preferences is by creating a Facebook group on a topic, using LinkedIn groups for the same purpose, or creating an email chain. This process also serves to create more exposure for your course. Because Udemy takes 50% of any tuition from a student whom they direct towards your course, you are going to want to invite people from your own circles in order to get 100% tuition from your sales.

Top Tip 2: Continue Your Communication through the Entire Production Process

After you've gotten your answers about which type of course would be the most popular, don't stop communicating in these circles. You can use the email marketing techniques from chapter 4 to help you keep interest in your course strong. This involves answering questions, monitoring feedback, and developing ways to gather new email address for your readership. If you skip this step, you're liable to lose valuable interest in your product and therefore customers and money.

Top Tip 3: Create Multiple Courses

Just like with any type of skill or sport, it is unlikely that your first course is going to be your best. Consider implementing tips 1 and 2 for multiple courses at once in order to learn by experience.

Top Tip 4: Create Free Courses

Yes, it's true. In order to build a significant following on Udemy, you would benefit from creating free course material. By exposing yourself and what you can offer through free content, people are more likely to establish trust with you. Once that trust is established, it is more likely that a student will purchase a course from you.

Top Tip 5: Produce YouTube Videos

While we will discuss how to make passive income through the production of YouTube videos in a separate chapter, publishing YouTube videos about your course may be just the tease you need to get people to buy your course. Additionally, a great way to entice people through a YouTube video is to offer a discount code at the end of the video. You are sure to drum up some business if people think that your course is offering a sale or can be considered a bargain.

It is important to understand from this chapter that Udemy can be a profitable passive income method given that the proper marketing methods are utilizing from the beginning. If you don't properly promote your course and figure out what people are interested in learning about, your course will sit on the Udemy site with little to no subscription. Because Udemy's terms are reasonable from a profit perspective, a little marketing legwork can go a long way. Plus, as with most forms of passive income, once you have established your following, it becomes easier to earn money with less work involved as time goes on.

Chapter 8:
Drop Shipping

While the previous chapter discussed how to make passive income through a service rather than a product, this chapter focuses on how to make a profit by making how you get your products to your customers more efficient. One way that savvy online sellers have found to make more money along their production line is through the implementation of drop shipping. This type of shipping can be contrasted to the shipping methods that were discussed in chapter 5 that revolved around setting up an account on Amazon FBA. In addition to making you even more money than through simply selling a product on a website, drop shipping takes away some of the headache surrounding preparing shipments for your customers. The most beneficial aspect to the processes of drop shipping is that you as the seller spend less time preparing an order for your customer, while still making a profit from shipping costs. Here we will take a look at how drop shipping works and how to maximally profit from this process.

How Drop Shipping Usually Works

The first condition that must be met before you drop ship anything to your customer is to understand that your online store must be selling something that can be drop shipped. This means that you are not selling a product that you make yourself. For example, let's pretend that your online store is in the business of selling patio furniture. If you have a woodworking shop and make all of your patio furniture yourself, the method of drop shipping would not work for you. Contrastingly, if you somehow get patio furniture from a brand name vendor at a wholesale price, you are considered a reseller. Typically, what happens is the vendor will ship you the orders at a discounted, wholesale price and then you take the items and ship them to your customer. This chain of sending the goods from one vendor to another is what constitutes many small businesses around the country. The process works, and it gives the reseller the opportunity to verify that the products he or she is selling are intact and correct before the products move to their final destination.

How You Can Benefit from Drop Shipping

If you have found a niche market for yourself online where the goods that you sell are simply being resold, then you have the opportunity to benefit from drop shipping your goods instead of shipping them yourself. If you do not find yourself in this category, feel free to skim your way over to the last chapter, chapter 9 about how to earn passive income through the production of YouTube videos.

Let's go back to our example about the patio furniture. Let's say that the house where you do most of your business is relatively small. It's unlikely that you will be able to store a lot of the patio furniture that you resell in your home at once. In order to prevent the possibility of having to replace your living room furniture with patio furniture, (could you imagine sleeping on a lounge chair every night?) you could reach out to companies who drop ship products to customers and make them do some of the legwork. A drop shipping company will provide the following services for you that will be included in the price that you pay them to drop ship your goods to your customer:

1. Finds the product in his or her stock. Instead of having to keep stock of your items, a drop shipping

service will make sure that the products you want drop shipped are received prior to shipment. In this way, the drop shipping service replaces of any type of warehouse need that your online marketplace has. In addition to finding the products in their stock, the drop shipping service also ensures that these products are reordered when stock runs out. This saves you time in multiple ways. It also eliminates the need for you to hold an inventory of goods even when no goods have been bought, keeping your money liquid instead of asset-oriented.

2. Packages your order. Shipping supplies are both costly and take up space. Because the drop shipper packages your goods for you, you don't have to worry about making sure that the product is being safely transported. Instead of spending your time learning about how to package goods effectively, you can spend more time focusing other areas, such as website aesthetics and reaching your marketing goals.

3. Generate invoices. If you spend enough time researching a good drop shipper, the company will even generate invoices with your company's name on it for you. If you find an exceptional drop shipper, they might even agree to add your logo to the invoice. Again, this saves you time in the sense that all you have to do is make sure that the customer's information is correct before placing the order, and the majority of the work is the responsibility of the drop shipper.

Of course, before deciding to invest your money into drop shipping services it is important to make sure that you can charge your customer more for shipping than the drop shipping service costs you. If you are not seeing a decent profit margin between the wholesale price of the good and your selling price, and the difference between what the drop shipper is charging you and what you are charging the customer for "you" to ship the product, this method will only prove to give you a headache without providing you with additional money. Because this way of earning passive income comes with the added bonus of handing responsibility to a third party, it is regarded as an extremely beneficial and relatively easy way to make money without much effort required.

Chapter 9:
YouTube – Making a Profit through Video Content

As with the previous ways we've looked at on how to earn passive income, the method of making money through the production of YouTube videos requires that you do some research before you set up your webcam. While most of the other methods that we've discussed have required research into external areas of interest, the starting point for this type of passive income begins in researching some aspects of yourself. Let's take a look at what types of questions you need to ask yourself to earn money through creating YouTube content, and then we will proceed to the details on how to make money on YouTube.

Where are Your Smarts?

Similar to the tactics used when trying to break into the Udemy field, the first step to understanding YouTube profitability is to ask yourself what you know. What processes do you understand that other people would potentially enjoy developing for themselves? In contrast to Udemy, this type of knowledge does not need to necessarily be on a topic that requires an entire course load of work behind it. Instead, it can be something much simpler and less time consuming. For example, let's say that as a side project you spend time repairing cracked iPhone screens. This could be a great topic to produce videos about because there is a need for this type of instruction online. Instead of paying someone to fix an iPhone screen for $100 or more, many people would prefer to do it themselves. Another question to ask yourself during this preliminary process is what type of knowledge have you most valued in the past? Again, in looking at our iPhone example, it becomes obvious that this type of information is both useful and valuable to the consumer.

How to Make Money from your YouTube Video

While it's important to know where to start before making a YouTube video for profit, you're really here to learn the secrets on how to make money on YouTube. The most important fact to remember when pursuing this goal is that while YouTube was created by three people who previously worked for PayPal, it was bought by Google in February of 2005. With this knowledge, it is obvious that the most beneficial practices when navigating the profitability of YouTube involve using other Google-owned enterprises. Let's look more into exactly what this means.

1. Keyword searches are still important. As with the other types of niche marketing that we've already gone over, figuring out which keywords are being Googled most frequently within a niche subject is still a top priority if you want to start earning money on YouTube.

2. Video optimization. When creating a video with the intention of uploading it to YouTube, you should definitely avoid uploading it directly to YouTube from the video program that you're using. Instead, you should save it as a file on your desktop, *and then* upload the file to YouTube. The reason for this is that the original file name is something that is not decipherable. To the average eye, the file name looks like a compilation of random numbers and

letters. Google cares about what you name your file from the perspective of YouTube. For our example, this means that the file name for your video on how to fix a cracked iPhone screen would read something similar to, "how-to-fix-cracked-iPhone-screen". You can see how the keywords that people would search on this topic correspond to the video file name. A common mistake that beginner YouTubers make is naming their file incorrectly. In addition to this, make sure to optimize your description. This involves making sure that your description of the video explains how to fix the problem too. That way, if people don't have time to watch your video, the video is still being helpful to the person in some way.

3. Turn ads on. In order to maximize your income, you need to turn ads on for your video. Google owns AdSense, so this will be the platform with which you'll be working. This how Google makes money through you. If you forget to turn your ads on, you'll be less likely to rank high within the keyword search on the niche topic you choose. This means you'll have less viewers, meaning that less ads will be seen, and ultimately means you will be less profitable.

While this chapter focused mostly on how to configure the technology surrounding your video, other important aspects of YouTube video production include practicing techniques that are needed while you're on the video. You need to make sure that you are somewhat prepared on the topic you're going to be teaching about prior to being seen on camera. Of course, you don't need to prepare a script word-for-word, but a general outline on your topic will be handy while on set. Practice what you are going to say multiple times before recording it. It might help to even set up the camera in front of you while you practice, because sometimes the camera's presence is enough to make you initially feel nervous. Additionally, remember that you're not filming a segment for Fox News or CNN. Your content doesn't have to be presented in a formal way. Lastly, edit your content. As applications such as Instagram and Photoshop have proven to the world, people enjoy visual media more when its manicured and pretty. Keep the video as short as possible, follow these techniques, and you'll be making a name for yourself on the YouTube stage in no time.

Conclusion

Thank you again for downloading this book!

I hope this book was able to help you to better understand how to start earning passive income. As you can see, there are multiple ways in which passive income can be available to you. Regardless of which method you choose to pursue, it is important to remember that the term "passive" in the phrase passive income does not necessarily mean that there is no work involved. Prepare yourself to put in the effort from the start, have patience, and understand the risks involved with starting any type of business. Most of these methods require some sort of startup cost, and you don't want to spend your money fruitlessly. If you follow the guidelines presented in this book, maybe one day you'll be able to sit back and watch as your passive revenue streams grow.

The next step is to keep researching how to make money by implementing passive revenue strategies. This book presented the basics. There is so much for you to continue learning, and this book is the tip of the ice burg. Additionally, it is ill-advised for you to attempt all of these strategies at once. Similar to when you research website niches to find a place for your website within a broader subject matter, you too should look for you your niche within the passive income market.

Finally, if you enjoyed this book, please take the time to share your thoughts and post a review on Amazon. It'd be greatly appreciated!

Thank you and good luck!

Discover how to make money without the drag of having to sit in a cubicle or in front of a computer all day. What if someone told you this was possible and you could make money even when you weren't working? Download *Passive Income: Learn to Easily Make Passive Money Online and Quit Your Job! Utilize Multiple Income Streams to Pay Off Debt and Become Financially Free* now to find out exciting ways to start making money that depend on you being your own boss. What's more, without a superior telling you what to do and when to do it, you'll create your own schedule. If you develop creative ways to make money with the techniques that are described in this book, you'll be ditching your co-workers and that copy machine that drives you nuts in no time.

It's no secret that most of us would love to spend our time traveling, bettering ourselves, or even sleeping instead of spending the majority of our time making money through avenues that are not always the most personally satisfying. Secrets that are less widely known that are available to you when you download this book include discovering exactly what type of characteristics you need to possess in order to start earning passive income. This includes decisive and invaluable advice on how to successfully begin this journey through the development of niche websites, email and affiliate marketing, Amazon FBA, Kindle publishing, YouTube video production, and more. What are you waiting for? Download *Passive Income: Learn to Easily Make Passive Money Online and Quit Your Job! Utilize Multiple Income Streams to Pay Off Debt and Become Financially Free* now. This is the go-to book for anyone interested in earning more without picking up a part time job. With this handy book, you'll be sipping mojitos on an exotic beach during working hours in no time.

You're guaranteed to learn:

- The demeanor necessary to operate passive business operation

- How to earn passive income through the maintenance of niche websites, emailing and affiliate marketing

- The insides of working with Amazon FBA

- Kindle E-book writing and how to maximize your profits in this field

- How to create online courses that people will be itching to buy

- How to make money through the production of YouTube videos

www.ingramcontent.com/pod-product-compliance
Lightning Source LLC
Chambersburg PA
CBHW070414190526
45169CB00003B/1257